It's a Jungle Out There

Gorilla Business Quotations

COMPILED & ILLUSTRATED
BY BRUCE GOODMANSEN

GIBBS·SMITH
➔P
PUBLISHER

SALT LAKE CITY

97 96 95 94   10 9 8 7 6 5 4 3 2 1

Introduction and compilation copyright © 1994 by Bruce Goodmansen

This is a Peregrine Smith Book, published by

Gibbs Smith, Publisher
P.O. Box 667
Layton, Utah 84041

Printed and bound in the United States of America

Library of Congress Cataloging-in Publication Data

It's a jungle out there : gorilla business quotations / [compiled] by Bruce Goodmansen.
  p. cm.
ISBN 0-87905-625-8
1. Business—Quotations, maxims, etc. I. Goodmansen, Bruce. II. Title: It is a jungle
out there. III. Title: Gorilla business quotations.
PN6084. B87I88 1994
808.88'2—dc20   93-50587

                                                         CIP

CONTENTS

———

INTRODUCTION

Thoughts rule the world.
Emerson

Successful professionals have something in common. All have been, and are, deeply motivated by the thoughts of sages past and present. Realize, now, I'm not referring to the numerous musty and unimaginative writings that are as useful to the mind as a bad case of chiggers is to the sensitive fanny. No, it's the gorilla-type quotes that inspire the great ones.

Gorilla business quotations are no-nonsense, compact, extremely powerful and rare. Their bite is incisive. Their ambiance is commanding. Muscular, hard-hitting, red-blooded, in-your-face, don't-mess-with-me, and suasively eloquent. That's the nature of the gorilla quote.

Herein you'll find the finest library of business wit and wisdom relating to your life and the life of your business. Thousands of quotes were reviewed. Only the most commanding were selected—each one a bona fide gorilla.

Now it's hard to ignore the message of a gorilla when it wants to make a point. The consequences may be dreadful to the loon who tries. Ignoring the wisdom found in this collection can be equally dire. So if you work for a living, buy yourself a banana, grab your book of Gorilla Business Quotations, find a quiet niche in the Jungle of Business, and relish the expedition within.

Bruce Goodmansen

Murphy's Law

He who limps is still walking.

Stanislaw J. Lec

God will not look you over
for medals, degrees
or diplomas, but for scars.
Elbert Hubbard

Remember your past mistakes
just long enough to profit by them.
Dan McKinnon

The real winners in life
are the losers who keep trying.
Anonymous

Whenever I make a bum decision,
I just go out and make another one.
Harry S. Truman

A patient mind
is the best remedy for trouble.
Plautus

A man is not finished when he's defeated;
he's finished when he quits.
Richard Milhous Nixon

I have had many troubles in my life,
but the worst of them never came.
James A. Garfield

Even God cannot change the past.
Agathon

A failure is a man who has blundered,
but is not able to cash in on the experience.
Elbert Hubbard

Experience is the name everyone
gives to their mistakes.

Oscar Wilde

For all sad words of tongue or pen,
the saddest are these: "It might have been."

John Greenleaf Whittier

Hardball Capitalism

Everyone lives by selling something.

Robert Louis Stevenson

A Quality Product
+ Unsurpassed Service
+ Common Sense^2 =
A Business Sensation

Simple Business Mathematics

Drive thy business,
let not that drive thee.

Benjamin Franklin

If profits are evil,
losses must be ten times worse.

Bertram Troy

Most salesmen try to take the horse to
water and make him drink.
Your job is to make the horse thirsty.

Gabriel M. Siegel

Professionals built the Titanic—amateurs the Ark.
Anonymous

Never burn a bridge
that connects you to a source of business,
unless the source is corrupt, for
fate may direct you to cross it again.
A bridge left standing costs nothing to rebuild.
Bruce Goodmansen

No nation was ruined by trade.
Benjamin Franklin

Don't forget until it's too late
that the business of life
is not business but living.

B. C. Forbes

True artists ship.
Steven Jobs

We're a nonprofit organization.
We didn't mean to be—but we are.
American Business Humor

Buy whatever kids are selling
on card tables in their front yards.
H. Jackson Brown, Jr.

If you are going to be a successful
duck hunter, you must go where the ducks are.
Paul "Bear" Bryant

It is far easier to sell a solution to a problem
than to sell a positive benefit.
Jay Conrad Levinson

The Apex Alpha Parameter

Always do right.
This will surprise some
people and
astonish the rest.

Mark Twain

This above all;
to thine own self be true,
And it must follow,
as the night the day,
Thou canst not then be false
to any man.

William Shakespeare

If the world goes against truth, then
Athanasius goes against the world.
Saint Athanasius

Only the disciplined are free.
James C. Penney

When the going gets tough,
the tough get going.
A Competitor's Maxim

It matters not how strait the gate,
How charged with punishments the scroll,
I am the master of my fate;
I am the captain of my soul.

William Ernest Henley

The ultimate measure of a man
is not where he stands in moments
of comfort but where he stands at times
of challenge and controversy.

Martin Luther King, Jr.

An honest man's word
is as good as his bond.

Miguel De Cervantes

The force of his own merit
makes his way.

William Shakespeare

Character is what God and the
angels know of us; reputation is what
men and women think of us.

Horace Mann

To know what is right
and not do it is
the worst cowardice.

Confucius

Great men have four
things in common:
They speak softly, have the
capacity for hard work,
a deep conviction for their cause
and a consuming belief in
their ability to do it.

John D. Hess

For as he thinketh in his heart, so is he.
The Bible

Not in the clamor of the crowded street,
Not in the shouts and plaudits of the throng,
But in ourselves, our triumph and defeat.
Henry Wadsworth Longfellow

When thou enter a city abide by its customs.
The Talmud

C O U R A G E

Pseudo Phobia

The first and great commandment is: Don't let them scare you.

Elmer Davis

Cowards die many times before their
deaths; the valiant never taste
of death but once.
William Shakespeare

Deep faith eliminates fear.
Lech Walesa

Courage is . . . grace under pressure.
Ernest Hemingway

Have not I commanded thee?
Be strong and of good courage;
be not afraid, neither be thou
dismayed: for the Lord thy God is
with thee withersoever thou goest.

The Bible

To carry care to bed is to sleep
with a pack on your back.
Thomas C. Haliburton

A ship in a harbor is safe,
but that is not what ships are built for.
John A. Shedd

Our doubts are traitors, And make us
lose the good we oft might win,
By fearing to attempt.

William Shakespeare

Nothing in life is to be feared.
It is only to be understood.

Marie Curie

E D U C A T I O N

Wisdomology

Chance favors the trained mind.

Louis Pasteur

In a time of drastic change, it is the learners who inherit the future. The learned find themselves equipped to live in a world that no longer exists.

Eric Hoffer

I read for three things: first, to know what the world has done during the last twenty-four hours, and is about to do today; second, for the knowledge that I specially want in my work; and third, for what will bring my mind into a proper mood.

Henry Ward Beecher

You don't learn anything
the second time
you're kicked by a mule.

Anonymous

You can see a lot by observing.

Yogi Berra

Ignorance is a voluntary misfortune.

Nicholas Ling

No matter what your occupation,
your chief occupation is to always
be a student.

Francis Bacon

When you're green, you're growing.
When you're ripe, you rot.

Ray Kroc

If you think education is expensive,
try ignorance.

Derek Bok

Learning for the mere sake of learning
is sterile. It's a form of play. For any
kind of learning to have meaning, it must not
only be capable of utilization, it must be used.
Unused learning is fertilizer left in the sack.

Tom Hopkins

Education is what a fellow gets by
reading the fine print, and experience is
what he gets by not reading it.

Anonymous

LEADERSHIP

Alpha Parameter II

When I want to know what France is thinking, I ask myself.

Charles de Gaulle

Anyone can hold the helm
when the sea is calm.
Publilius Syrus

Leaders are movers and shakers,
original, inventive, unpredictable,
imaginative, full of surprises that
discomfit the enemy in war and
the main office in peace.
Hugh Nibley

We will either find a way or make one.

Hannibal—on crossing the Alps

If you have no enemies, you are apt
to be in the same predicament
in regard to friends.

Elbert Hubbard

One good head is better than
a hundred strong hands.

Thomas Fuller

We know the mistake of doing nothing
from our own experience.
Mikhail Gorbachev

Leadership is the capacity to
translate vision into reality.
Warren G. Bennis

Most companies have room for only one
or two "generalists." And they're usually
called chairman or president.
Mark H. McCormack

The achievement of excellence can occur only if the organization promotes a culture of creative dissatisfaction.

Lawrence M. Miller

The conventional definition of management is getting work done through people, but real management is developing people through work.

Agha Hasan Abedi

L   I   F   E

The Human Condition

Life is either daring adventure or nothing.

Helen Keller

Life is uncertain. Eat dessert first!

Sol Gordon & Harold Brecher

When you get to the end of your rope,
tie a knot and hang on. And swing!

Leo Buscaglia

Sometimes it is more important to discover what one cannot do, than what one can do.
Lin Yutang

Begin at once to live, and count each separate day as a separate life.
Lucius Annaeus Seneca

Most of us spend our lives as if we had another one in the bank.
Ben Irwin

All life is an experiment.
Oliver Wendell Holmes, Jr.

But men must know, that in this
theater of man's life it is reserved
only for God and the angels
to be lookers on.
Francis Bacon

Action is the antidote to despair.

Joan Baez

A life at ease is a difficult pursuit.

William Cowper

He who is not busy being born
is busy dying.

Bob Dylan

OPPORTUNITY

A Blessing From Fate

Everything starts as somebody's daydream.

Larry Niven

The Chinese use two brush strokes
to write the word "crisis."
One brush stroke stands for danger;
the other for opportunity.

Richard Milhous Nixon

The creation of a thousand forests
is in one acorn.

Ralph Waldo Emerson

Circumstances? I make circumstances!
Napoleon Bonaparte

*If your ship doesn't come in,
swim out to it!*
Jonathan Winters

*There is no security on this earth;
there is only opportunity.*
Douglas MacArthur

The trouble with opportunity is that
it always comes disguised
as hard work.

Herbert V. Prochnow, Sr.

A wise man makes more
opportunities than he finds.

Francis Bacon

We are told that talent creates
its own opportunities.
But it sometimes seems that intense
desire creates not only its own
opportunities, but its own talents.

Eric Hoffer

OPPOSITION

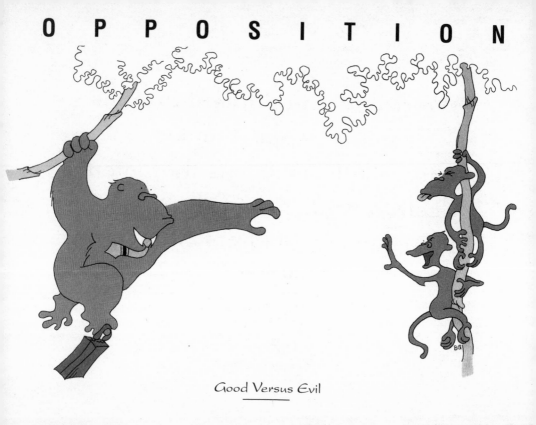

Good Versus Evil

Every normal man must
be tempted, at times,
to spit on his hands,
hoist the black flag, and
begin slitting throats.

H. L. Mencken

The breakfast of champions is not cereal, it's the opposition.
Nick Seitz

Suppose Edison's parents had taught him contentment.
Clarence Day, Jr.

It is better to bend than to break.
Aesop

What on earth would a man do
with himself if something did not
stand in his way?

H. G. Wells

There comes a time in the affairs of
man when he must take the bull
by the tail and face the situation.

W. C. Fields

The nearer the dawn
the darker the night.

Henry Wadsworth Longfellow

If there are obstacles, the shortest
line between two points may be
the crooked one.

Bertolt Brecht

There are no gains without pains.
Adlai Stevenson

A clay pot sitting in the sun will always be a clay pot. It has to go through the white heat of the furnace to become porcelain.
Mildred Struven

P A S S I O N

Spirtiual Furor

Success demands more than a good idea. It demands fanatical devotion.

Mortimer Levitt

Only the passions, only great passions, can elevate the mind to great things.
Denis Diderot

Never say die.
Charles Dickens

Nothing great was ever achieved
without enthusiasm.
Ralph Waldo Emerson

Every time you approach a task,
you should be aiming to do the best job that's
ever been done and not stop until you've
done it. Anyone who does that will be
successful—and rich.
David Ogilvy

Do or do not.
There is no try.

Yoda

We may affirm absolutely
that nothing great in the world
has ever been accomplished
without passion.

George Wilhelm Hegel

One person with a belief is a social power
equal to ninety-nine who have only interests.
John Stuart Mill

If you aren't fired with enthusiasm,
you will be fired with enthusiasm.
Vince Lombardi

Genius is initiative on fire.

Holbrook Jackson

Without passion man is a mere latent force
and possibility, like the flint
which awaits the shock of the iron
before it can give forth its spark.

Henri Frederic Amiel

Production Before Production

The ultimate inspiration is the deadline.

Nolan Bushnell

If you do not know to which port you are sailing, no wind is favorable.
Lucius Annaeus Seneca

When a decision has been made and the die is cast, then murder the alternatives.
Emory S. Adams, Jr.

Adventure is the result of poor planning.
Blatchford Snell

Ah, but a man's reach should exceed
his grasp, Or what's a Heaven for?
Robert Browning

Don't bunt. Aim out of the ball park.
Aim for the company of immortals.
David Ogilvy

To live only for some future goal is shallow.
It's the sides of the mountain that
sustains life, not the top.
Robert Pirsig

Make no little plans.
They have no magic to stir
men's blood.
Make big plans: aim high
in hope and work.

D. H. Burnham

It will not always be summer:
build barns.
Hesiod

The best way to predict the future
is to invent it.
Alan Kay

Excellence in Forte

The best ad is a good product.

Alan H. Meyer

When a thing is thoroughly well done
it often has the air of being a miracle.
Arnold Bennett

I am easily satisfied with the best.
Winston Churchill

Never buy a saddle
until you have met the horse.
Mortimer B. Zuckerman

I have lived in this world just long
enough to look carefully
the second time into things that
I am the most certain of
the first time.

Josh Billings

A man would do nothing
if he waited until he could do it so well
that no one could find fault.

John Henry Newman

For want of a nail the shoe was lost;
For want of a shoe the horse was lost;
For want of a horse the rider was lost;
For want of a rider the battle was lost;
All for want of care about a horseshoe nail.

Benjamin Franklin

In the race for quality, there is no finish line.
David T. Kearns

Whatever is worth doing at all is
worth doing well.
Lord Chesterfield

What is easy is seldom excellent.
Samuel Johnson

REALITY

Catalyst to Truth

There are few things
as uncommon
as common sense.

Frank McKinney Hubbard

The difference between
the impossible and the possible
lies in a person's determination.
Tommy Lasorda

A little rebellion now and then
is a good thing.
Thomas Jefferson

The dogmas of the quiet past are inadequate
to the stormy present.
Abraham Lincoln

To live is to change, and to be perfect is to have changed often.

John Henry Newman

No one can make you feel small without your consent.

Eleanor Roosevelt

Any concern too small to be turned into a prayer is too small to be made into a burden.

Corrie ten Boom

R **I** **S** **K**

Exposure to Adventure

There's as much risk in doing nothing as in doing something.

Tammell Crow

Live dangerously. Build your
cities on the slopes of Vesuvius.

Fredrich Nietzsche

I don't know where speculation
got a bad name, since I know of
no forward leap which was not
fathered by speculation.

John Steinbeck

Progress means taking risks,
for you can't steal home and
keep your foot on third base.

Herbert V. Prochnow

Behold the turtle: He only makes
progress when he sticks his neck out.

James Bryant Conant

Take a chance!
All life is a chance.
The man who goes furthest
is generally the one who
is willing to do and dare.

Dale Carnegie

The pioneers got all the arrows.

Burt Lance

Three things are good in
little measures
and evil in large:
yeast, salt, and hesitation.

The Talmud

S E R V I C E

Artful Assistance

Treat the customer as an appreciating asset.

Tom Peters

I have more fun and enjoy more financial success when I stop trying to get what I want and start helping other people get what they want.

Spencer Johnson

Only a life lived for others is a life worth living.

Albert Einstein

The free market is in accordance with the golden rule. We advance ourselves as we help others. The more we help others, the more we receive in return.

Percy Greaves, Jr.

I don't know what your destiny will be, but one thing I know: the only ones among you who will be really happy are those who have sought and found how to serve.

Albert Schweitzer

I read in a book that a man called Christ went about doing good. It is most disconcerting to me to find that I am so easily content with just going about.

Toyohiko Kagawa

A man's true wealth is the good he does in the world.

Mohammed

Give a man a fish and you will feed him forone day.
Teach a man to fish and you feed him for a lifetime.

Chinese Proverb

Be ashamed to die until you have won
some victory for humanity.
Horace Mann

Consumers are statistics.
Customers are people.
Stanly Marcus

S I M P L I C I T Y

Synonym for a Child

If people concentrated on the really important things in life, there'd be a shortage of fishing poles.

Doug Larson

Think

IBM Motto

Play so that you may be serious.
Anacharsis

Sometimes when I consider what tremendous consequences come from little things—a chance word, a tap on the shoulder, or a penny dropped on a newsstand—I am tempted to think . . . there are no little things.

Bruce Barton

All the really good ideas I ever had
came to me while I was milking a cow.
Grant Wood

Nothing is more simple than greatness;
indeed to be simple is to be great.
Ralph Waldo Emerson

Happiness is not a station that you arrive at,
but a manner of traveling.
Margaret Lee Runbeck

Happiness means quiet nerves.

W. C. Fields

It has long been an axiom of mine
that the little things are infinitely
the most important.

Sherlock Holmes (Arthur Conan Doyle)

Always remember
that this whole thing was started
by a mouse.

Walt Disney

S U C C E S S

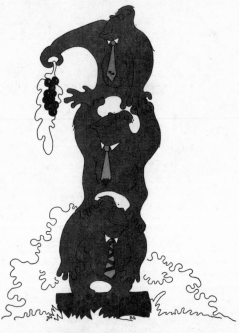

Sans the Misery Index

When you win, nothing hurts.

Joe Namath

The only justification of rebellion is success.
Thomas Brackett Reed

What's money? A man is a success if he gets
up in the morning and gets to
bed at night and in between does
what he wants to do.
Bob Dylan

Our greatest weakness
lies in giving up.
The most certain way to succeed
is to always try just one more time.

Thomas Edison

The pessimist complains about the wind; the optimist expects it to change; the realist adjusts the sails.

William Arthur Ward

The first rule of winning: Don't beat yourself.

A Competitor's Axiom

The secret of success
is constancy to purpose.

Benjamin Disraeli

The surest way not to fail is to
determine to succeed.

Roger Babson

To be a champ you have to believe in
yourself when nobody else will.

Sugar Ray Robinson

No one knows what he can do
till he tries.
Publilius Syrus

Many people dream of success.
To me success can only be achieved through
repeated failure and introspection.
In fact, success represents the 1 percent
of your work which results from
the 99 percent that is called failure.
Soichiro Honda

Some men have thousands
of reasons why they cannot do
what they want to do,
when all they need is one reason
why they can.
Dr. Willis R. Whitney

There are no shortcuts
to any place worth going.
Beverly Sills

T   I   M   E

Precious Commodity

Seize the day and put the least possible trust in tomorrow.

Horace

I am glad the eight-hour day
had not been invented when I was
a young man.
Thomas A. Edison

A man who dares to
waste an hour of time has not
discovered the value of life.
Charles Darwin

Better three hours too soon than
a minute too late.

William Shakespeare

Whenever you see a job to do,
ask yourself these two questions:
If not by me—by whom?
If not now—when?

Arthur Lageux

He who hesitates is lost.

Anonymous

I would willingly stand at street corners, hat in hand, begging passers-by to drop their unused minutes into it.

Bernard Berenson

No one ever got very far by
working a 40-hour week.
Most of the notable people I know
are trying to manage a 40-hour day.

Channing Pollock

The fool with all his other faults,
has this also, he is always
getting ready to live.

Epictetus

U N I Q U E N E S S

Peculiar to the Peculiar

You see things and
you say "Why?"
But I dream things that
never were,
and say "Why not?"

George Bernard Shaw

I stand on my desk to remind myself that we must constantly force ourselves to look at things differently.

N. H. Kleinbaum

If a man does not keep pace with his companions, perhaps it is because he hears a different drummer.

Henry David Thoreau

To be nobody-but-myself—in a world which is doing its best, night and day, to make you everybody else—means to fight the hardest battle which any human being can fight, and never stop fighting.

e. e. cummings

The reasonable man adapts himself to the world; the unreasonable one persists in trying to adapt the world to himself. Therefore, all progress depends on the unreasonable man.

George Bernard Shaw

Humanity's most valuable assets have been the non-conformists. Were it not for the non-conformists, he who refuses to be satisfied to go along with the continuance of things as they are, and insists upon attempting to find new ways of bettering things, the world would have known little progress indeed.

Josiah William Gitt

Two roads diverged in a wood,
and J—J took the one less traveled by,
And that has made all the difference.

Robert Frost

The heights by great men reached and kept,
Were not attained by sudden flight,
But they, while their companions slept,
Were toiling upward in the night.

Henry Wadsworth Longfellow

Is it so bad then to be misunderstood?
Pythagoras was misunderstood, and Socrates, and
Jesus, and Luther, and Copernicus, and Galileo,
and Newton, and every pure and wise spirit that
ever took flesh. To be great is to be misunderstood.

Ralph Waldo Emerson

Mightier than Excalibur

To hold a pen
is to be at war.

Voltaire

You will always find some Eskimos
ready to instruct the Congolese on
how to cope with heat waves.
Stanislaw J. Lec

When you give advice, remember that
Socrates was a Greek philosopher
who went around giving good advice.
They poisoned him.
Anonymous

Advice to speakers: If you don't strike oil in
twenty minutes, stop boring.
Adam S. Bennion

Perhaps Hell is nothing more than an
enormous conference of those who, with little
or nothing to say, take an eternity to say it.
Dudley C. Stone

It usually takes me more than three weeks to
prepare a good impromptu speech.
Mark Twain

To speak of "mere words" is much like speaking of "mere dynamite."

C. J. Ducasse

If everybody thought before they spoke, the silence would be deafening.

Gerald Barzan

The trouble with most of us is
that we would rather be ruined by praise
than saved by criticism.
Norman Vincent Peale

Thunder is good, thunder is impressive;
but it is lightning that does the work.
Mark Twain

W O R K

Foreplay to Leisure

Genius is one
per cent inspiration
and ninety-nine
per cent perspiration.

Thomas Edison

Never confuse motion with action.
Ernest Hemingway

Three people were at work on a construction site. All were doing the same job, but when asked what his job was, the answer varied. "Breaking rocks," the first replied. "Earning my living," the second said. "Helping to build a cathedral," said the third.

Peter Schultz

The difficult is done at once;
the impossible takes a little longer.
Armed Forces Motto

The beginning is half of every action.
Greek Proverb

Work spares us from three great evils:
boredom, vice and need.
Voltaire

The harder you work, the luckier you get.
Gary Player

The hardest work of all: Doing nothing.
Malcolm Forbes

The journey of a thousand miles
begins with one step.
Lao-tse

There's always free cheese in a mouse trap.
Anonymous

God sells us all things at the price of labor.

Leonardo da Vinci

Thank God every morning when
you get up that you have something
to do that day which must be done whether
you like it or not.

Charles Kingsley

It is better to wear out than to rust out.

Richard Cumberland

The outlook of our country lies in
the quality of its idleness.
Irwin Edman

All these writers of economics
overrate the importance of work.
Every man has a profound instinct
that idleness is the true reward of work,
even if it only comes at the end of life.
William Yeats